W9-ARL-385

DISCOVER BABY ANIMALS
Bear Cub

Written by Sarah Toast

Illustrated by Krista Brauckmann-Towns

Copyright © 1997 Publications International, Ltd.
All rights reserved. This publication may not be reproduced or quoted
in whole or in part by any means whatsoever without written permission from

Louis Weber, C.E.O.
Publications International, Ltd.
7373 North Cicero Avenue
Lincolnwood, Illinois 60646

Permission is never granted for commercial purposes.

Manufactured in U.S.A.

ISBN: 0-7853-2348-1

PUBLICATIONS INTERNATIONAL, LTD.
Rainbow Books is a trademark of Publications International, Ltd.

As summer draws to an end, Mother Bear roams through the mountain forest, gathering and eating enormous amounts of berries and fruit.

Mother Bear is putting on fat so she can sleep the entire winter. The layer of fat will keep her warm and help her provide rich milk for the baby bear that will be born.

👣 FUN FACT

Teddy bears were first known as Teddy's bears, named for President Theodore Roosevelt after he refused to shoot a young black bear in 1902.

Mother Bear chooses a rocky cave to be her den during the winter. Inside the den, she and her baby will be protected from the cold wind and blowing snow. She pads it with moss, leaves, and grass to make it warm and soft for herself and the baby.

As the first flakes of winter snow begin to fall, Mother Bear settles down and drifts off to sleep.

How long do bears live?
Bears can live up to 20 years in the wild.

In the middle of winter, when the snow drifts are deep outside the den, Mother Bear's tiny cub is born. With closed eyes and hardly any fur, the cub will grow quickly, nourished by Mother Bear's rich milk.

Baby Bear and Mother Bear sleep on, but Mother Bear will wake up and protect him if the winter home is disturbed.

👣 FUN FACT

A mother bear sits or lies on her side in her den and keeps her cub warm by cuddling him close to her body.

In a few weeks, Baby Bear's eyes open. He is now covered in thick, soft fur. Mother Bear and Baby Bear stay in their snug den another month.

In the spring, they emerge from the den. Mother Bear shows Baby Bear how to look through the forest for tender shoots that will make a good meal for them.

?

How long do bear cubs stay in the den?
Cubs stay in the den for three months before they venture outside. During these three months, they spend most of their time sleeping. They wake only to drink their mother's milk.

Mother Bear makes her way with Baby Bear down the grassy slope to the elks' winter range. She lifts up her head and sniffs the breeze. Baby Bear moves his raised head back and forth so hard that he falls right over.

Mother Bear finds an elk that died in the winter when the snows were deep and not enough food could be found.

🐾 FUN FACT

Bears have such small eyes that people often assume they also have poor eyesight, but bears probably see as well as many humans.

Mother Bear eats what she can of the nourishing elk meat. Then she buries it in a shallow hole and covers it with leaves, twigs, and dirt. She will return to it later.

Baby Bear learns by watching what his mother does. The most important rules for Baby Bear to learn are to follow mother, obey mother, and have fun.

How long do bear cubs stay with their mother?
Bear cubs stay with their mother about two years. During this time, they learn many survival tips, such as what to eat and how to escape predators, before they venture out on their own.

Mother Bear teaches her cub how to turn over fallen branches and look for food. With their claws, Baby Bear and Mother Bear dig up bulbs, roots, and snails.

When his mother stops to rest, Baby Bear climbs all over her. He somersaults into her lap and nibbles her ears, then runs off to chase a field mouse.

What do bears eat?
Bears will eat almost anything they can get their paws on, including grasses, berries, tree bark, plants, insects, some small mammals, and, of course, honey!

When Mother Bear looks up from playing with her cub, she sees that a lean wolf is watching them. Quickly she chases the Baby Bear into a hollow tree stump. Then she turns to face the wolf.

Mother Bear stands up on her hind legs, swings her front paws, and roars a loud growl. The wolf quickly runs away.

👣 FUN FACT

Bears have five claws on each foot. They use their front paws for catching and holding prey, digging for insects and roots, and climbing trees.

Mother Bear calls to her cub, but he doesn't come out of the hollow stump. Mother Bear goes to find out why.

Baby Bear has found a honeycomb with honey from last summer still inside. Baby Bear sticks his little paw in the honeycomb and then licks it. He tastes the wildflowers of summer in the sweet honey.

👣 FUN FACT

As the bear cub's first summer draws to an end, he is able to find his own food, although he might drink milk from Mother Bear occasionally. Now he must eat as much food as he can to prepare for his winter sleep.

When Baby Bear backs out of the hollow log, he brings some tasty honeycomb for his mother. She happily eats the honey, and then she and her cub give each other a true bear hug.